First Multiplication

5-7 years

Notes for grown-ups

- This book has been written to help your child develop their first maths skills. They will practise multiplying and dividing.

- The activities in this book are organized to build on what your child learned on the previous page. If they are finding something tricky, go back to a page they feel confident with.

- Some of the activities in this book require additional learning materials. You will need some dice, coloured pencils or crayons, and counters (you could use paper, little toys or buttons).

- Left-handed children should tilt the book so that the top left corner is higher than the right. The book should be slightly to the left of their bodies. This will help them to see their writing and avoid smudging.

- Look out for the **How are you doing?** sections. These give your child an opportunity to reflect on their progress and give you an idea of how your child is doing.

- Let your child check their own answers at the back of the book. Encourage them to talk about what they have learned.

Educational Consultant: Claire Hubbard.
With thanks to Child Autism UK, Pace, Amy Callaby and Jack Callaby.

Your Ladybird Class friends!

Zara Penguin loves all kinds of dance, as well as stories about princesses, knights and superheroes. Zara has cerebral palsy and wears an ankle-foot orthosis on each leg to help her walk. Her favourite lessons are history and circle time.

Nia Hedgehog is the newest member of Ladybird Class! She loves video games and skateboarding. Her favourite lessons are computing and geography.

Tao Meerkat wants to save the planet! He loves animals, nature and the environment. But he also likes magical stories and role-playing. His favourite lessons are science and phonics.

Olivia Crocodile always has lots of energy and is ready to change the world! She loves building things, and she has a red belt in karate. Her favourite lessons are maths and PE.

Noah Panda loves to craft, play on the computer and, most of all, he loves to bake. He collects lots of things like badges and pebbles. Noah is on the autism spectrum. His favourite lessons are art and playtime.

Ali Lion is quiet, but his head is full of daydreams and imagination. He loves to sing and to dress up in fancy costumes. His favourite lessons are literacy and music.

Contents

Counting caterpillars

Ali Lion wants to know exactly how many caterpillars are living on the leaves. Practise counting in 2s with Ali.

Ali Lion is counting the caterpillars in rows. Can you help him?

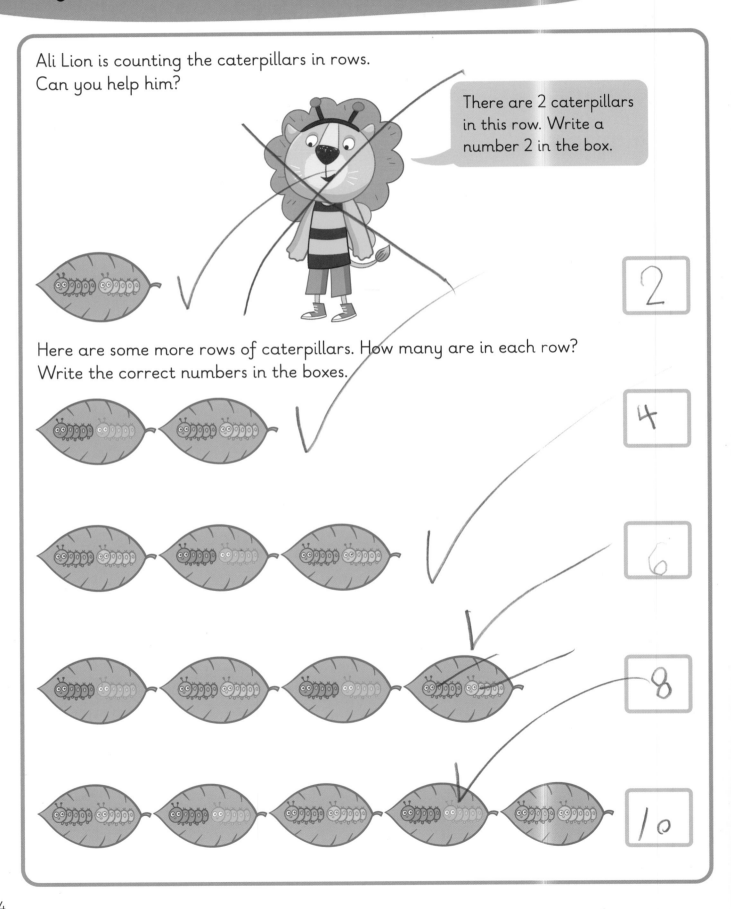

There are 2 caterpillars in this row. Write a number 2 in the box.

2

Here are some more rows of caterpillars. How many are in each row? Write the correct numbers in the boxes.

4

6

8

10

Zara Penguin has found a quicker way to count the caterpillars.

You don't need to count all the caterpillars each time. Can you see there are 3 lots of 2? We can count them in 2s.

Fill in the missing numbers in these lines, then read out all the numbers. When you say a number that is in a box, clap your hands.

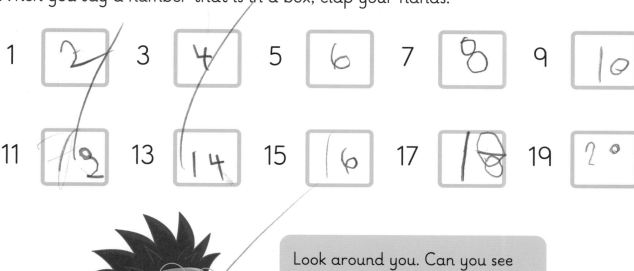

1 | 2 | 3 | 4 | 5 | 6 | 7 | 8 | 9 | 10

11 | 2 | 13 | 14 | 15 | 6 | 17 | 18 | 19 | 20

Look around you. Can you see things that come in 2s, like socks, shoes and gloves? Count them and clap your hands as you go.

How are you doing?

How are you feeling about counting in 2s?

- ☐ Great! I can't wait to show my friends how to count in 2s.
- ✓ I need a bit more help and practice before I can feel confident.

More counting in 2s

The friends in Ladybird Class love counting in 2s. They have created some fun challenges for you!

How many boots are there? Count up in 2s and write the numbers in the boxes.

How many gloves do Ladybird Class have altogether? Count in 2s to work it out.

There needs to be 2 buns in each bag. Count the buns, then work out how many bags Noah Panda will need.

How many pairs of socks does Ali Lion have? Draw a circle round each pair, then write the number.

| 2 | 4 | 6 | 8 | 10 | 12 | 14 | 16 | 18 | 20 |

We are counting in 2s again. Use the number line to help you.

We are going to work outside today. We need our wellies!

[ ] [ ]

It's cold today! We need our gloves.

[ ] [ ] [ ] [ ]

Look at all these buns I made! I need to put 2 buns in each bag.

[ ] [ ]

Noah will need [ ] bags.

A pair is a set of two things that are used together!

Ali has [ ] pairs of socks.

22   24   26   28   30   32   34   36   38   40

How many 2s?

Count along with Ladybird Class to find out about the 2 times table. Have fun!

Count the number of friends and the number of legs in each picture.

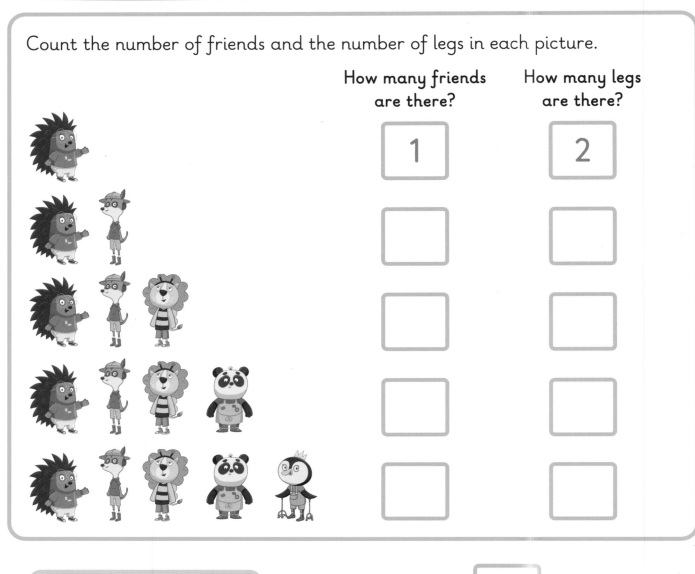

	How many friends are there?	How many legs are there?
	1	2

Did you complete the chart? Now fill in the missing numbers on this list.

1 friend has ☐ legs.

2 friends have ☐ legs.

3 friends have ☐ legs.

4 friends have ☐ legs.

5 friends have ☐ legs.

How many eyes do the friends have? 6 lots of 2 is 12. This is called **multiplying**.

We each have 2 eyes. So, there are 6 friends with 2 eyes each.

This is how we would write 6 lots of 2 as a number sentence.

We could say that 1 lot of 2 is 2, 2 lots of 2 is 4, and 3 lots of 2 is 6, and so on.

$$6 \times 2 = 12$$

This × sign means **multiply**, **lots of** or **times**.

See if you can finish off this pattern.

1 × 2 = ☐ 2

2 × 2 = ☐ 4

3 × 2 = ☐ 6

4 × 2 = ☐

5 × 2 = ☐

6 × 2 = ☐

7 × 2 = ☐

8 × 2 = ☐

9 × 2 = ☐

10 × 2 = ☐

11 × 2 = ☐

12 × 2 = ☐

This is called the 2 times table! We are multiplying numbers by 2.

You can play this game with lots of different things at home. Practise your 2 times table with pairs of shoes, or anything else that usually comes in a pair.

Counting in 5s

Ladybird Class are counting in 5s today. Join in!

Can you help Tao Meerkat count up in 5s? Count the petals, then fill in the numbers. Use the number line to help you.

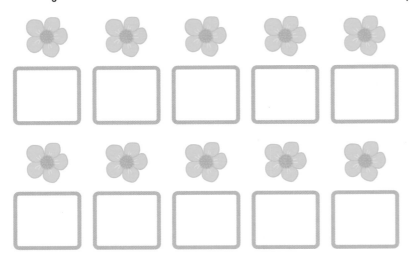

I love these buttercup flowers! There are 5 petals on each flower.

Can you see a pattern in these numbers? We could say that 1 lot of 5 is 5, 2 lots of 5 is 10, and so on.

There are 5 lots of 5 balloons. How many altogether?

$5 \times 5 =$ ☐

| 5 | 10 | 15 | 20 | 25 | 30 | 35 | 40 | 45 | 50 |

Do you remember the sign × means **lots of** or **times**?
See if you can finish off this pattern.

1 × 5 = [5]

2 × 5 = [10]

3 × 5 = [15]

4 × 5 = [   ]

5 × 5 = [   ]

6 × 5 = [   ]

7 × 5 = [   ]

8 × 5 = [   ]

9 × 5 = [   ]

10 × 5 = [   ]

11 × 5 = [   ]

12 × 5 = [   ]

This is called the 5 times table! We are multiplying numbers by 5.

How are you doing?

Are you getting the hang of multiplying in 2s and 5s now?

- [ ] Yes! I feel confident about the 2 and 5 times tables.
- [ ] I'd like help understanding it and some more practice.

55   60   65   70   75   80   85   90   95   100

The multiplying market

Practise your multiplication skills as you go shopping with Ladybird Class. Use your 2 and 5 times tables to help you.

Ladybird Class are buying trays of fruit and vegetables.

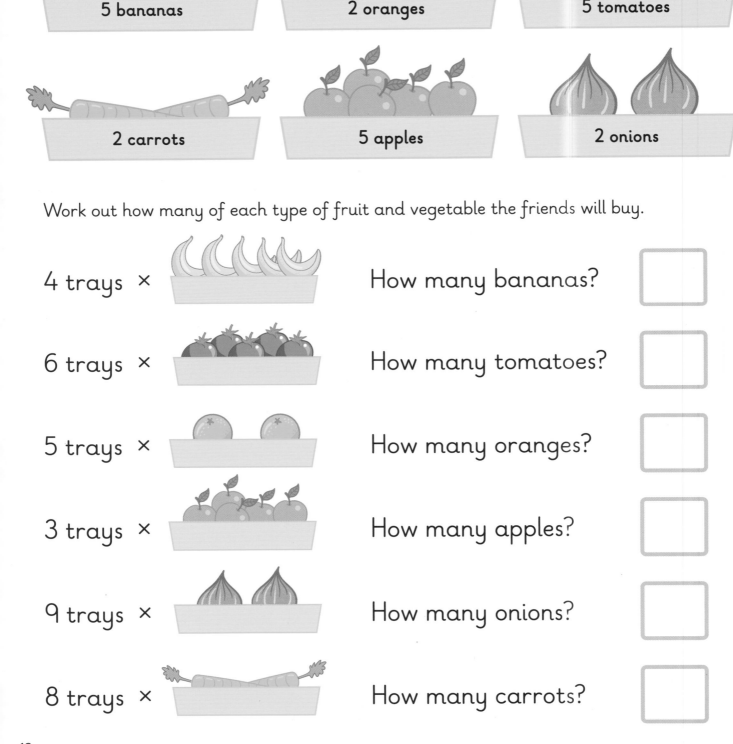

5 bananas

2 oranges

5 tomatoes

2 carrots

5 apples

2 onions

Work out how many of each type of fruit and vegetable the friends will buy.

4 trays × How many bananas? ☐

6 trays × How many tomatoes? ☐

5 trays × How many oranges? ☐

3 trays × How many apples? ☐

9 trays × How many onions? ☐

8 trays × How many carrots? ☐

After lunch, Ladybird Class buy ice creams for all their friends.

How much will these ice creams cost? Use your 2 and 5 times tables to help you.

Who has spent the most money? _____

The daisy-chain game

The friends in Ladybird Class have been busy making daisy chains. Each chain has 10 daisies in it.

How many daisies are there altogether? Count in 10s to find out.

10   20   30   40   50

The friends joined all their daisy chains together. What a long daisy chain!

Put a circle round daisy number 10.

This daisy is number 1!

This is daisy number 40. Draw a diamond round it.

Start

Which daisy is number 65? Draw a star round it.

Can you find daisy number 90? Put a box round it.

The last daisy is very special. What number is it?

Noah Panda's special number is ☐.

60   70   80   90   100

Mountain climbing

Practise counting in 2s, 5s and 10s as you race to the top of the mountain! Play with a friend or make two counters race each other.

How to play

1 You need two counters. Make your own with paper or use buttons or little toys. You will also need a dice.

2 Place the counters on **Start** and take turns rolling the dice to see how many spaces you can move forward.

3 When you land on a green ● number, go back to the start and count to that number in 2s. When you land on a pink ● number, go back to the start and count to that number in 5s. When you land on a yellow ● number, go back to the start and count to that number in 10s.

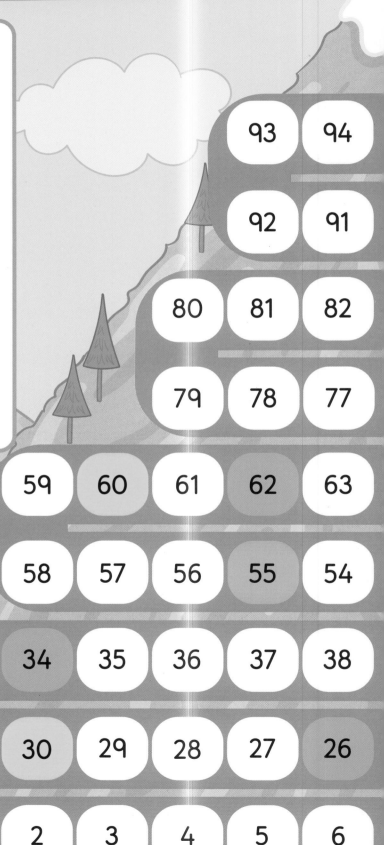

| 93 | 94 |
| 92 | 91 |

| 80 | 81 | 82 |
| 79 | 78 | 77 |

| 59 | 60 | 61 | 62 | 63 |
| 58 | 57 | 56 | 55 | 54 |

| 33 | 34 | 35 | 36 | 37 | 38 |
| 32 |
| 31 | 30 | 29 | 28 | 27 | 26 |

Start | 1 | 2 | 3 | 4 | 5 | 6 |

Finish

100

99

98

95 96 97

90 89 88 87

83 84 85 86

76 75 74 73 72 71

70

64 65 66 67 68 69

53 52 51 50 49 48 47

46

39 40 41 42 43 44 45

25 24 23 22 21 20 19 18 17

16

7 8 9 10 11 12 13 14 15

Number-line jumps

Join Ladybird Class as they play a jumping game! They are making jumps of 2, 5 and 10 along number lines.

How to play

1 You will need a dice.

2 Choose which number line to play first.

3 Throw the dice to see how many jumps you need to make along the number line. Remember to always start on 0.

4 Fill in the number sentences below your chosen number line.

5 When you finish your chosen number line, try the other two.

Cool! I've thrown a 6.

Then you need to make 6 jumps of 2. Remember to start on 0.

Make jumps of 2 along this number line, then fill in your jumping number sentences.

0   2   4   6   8   10   12

1 jump of 2 landed at ☐   1 × 2 = ☐

2 jumps of 2 landed at ☐   2 × 2 = ☐

3 jumps of 2 landed at ☐   3 × 2 = ☐

4 jumps of 2 landed at ☐   4 × 2 = ☐

5 jumps of 2 landed at ☐   5 × 2 = ☐

6 jumps of 2 landed at ☐   6 × 2 = ☐

Make jumps of 5 along this number line, then fill in your jumping number sentences.

0   5   10   15   20   25   30

1 jump of 5 landed at [ ]   1 × 5 = [ ]

2 jumps of 5 landed at [ ]   2 × 5 = [ ]

3 jumps of 5 landed at [ ]   3 × 5 = [ ]

4 jumps of 5 landed at [ ]   4 × 5 = [ ]

5 jumps of 5 landed at [ ]   5 × 5 = [ ]

6 jumps of 5 landed at [ ]   6 × 5 = [ ]

Make jumps of 10 along this number line, then fill in your jumping number sentences.

0   10   20   30   40   50   60

1 jump of 10 landed at [ ]   1 × 10 = [ ]

2 jumps of 10 landed at [ ]   2 × 10 = [ ]

3 jumps of 10 landed at [ ]   3 × 10 = [ ]

4 jumps of 10 landed at [ ]   4 × 10 = [ ]

5 jumps of 10 landed at [ ]   5 × 10 = [ ]

6 jumps of 10 landed at [ ]   6 × 10 = [ ]

Number patterns

Ladybird Class are using their multiplication skills to make number patterns. Join them to see what patterns appear!

Count in 2s, 5s and 10s on this 100 square. Follow the instructions to make different patterns.

How to play

When you count in 2s, colour in each number you land on.   2

When you count in 5s, circle each number you land on.   5

When you count in 10s, cross out the numbers you land on.   10

1	2	3	4	5	6	7	8	9	10
11	12	13	14	15	16	17	18	19	20
21	22	23	24	25	26	27	28	29	30
31	32	33	34	35	36	37	38	39	40
41	42	43	44	45	46	47	48	49	50
51	52	53	54	55	56	57	58	59	60
61	62	63	64	65	66	67	68	69	70
71	72	73	74	75	76	77	78	79	80
81	82	83	84	85	86	87	88	89	90
91	92	93	94	95	96	97	98	99	100

Look at the patterns you have made! Which numbers are marked three times? Write them here.

Can you help me to draw this lovely shell? Start on 2, then count in 2s to join the dots.

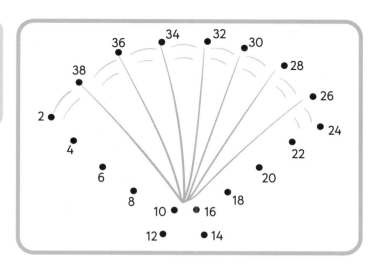

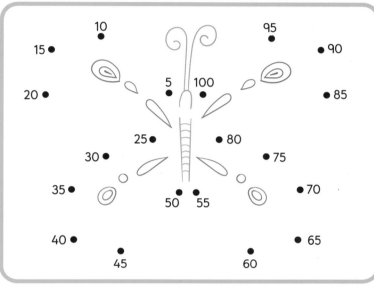

This butterfly looks just like one I saw today. Can you help me to draw it by counting in 5s?

Let's draw this dinosaur! Count in 10s to join the dots.

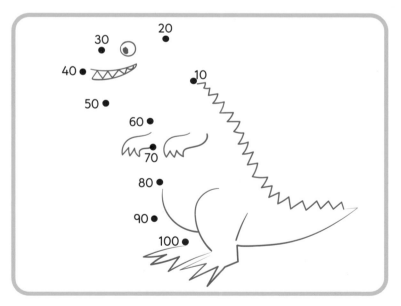

How are you doing?

How are you feeling about counting in 2s, 5s and 10s?

☐ I finished the patterns, and I could show a friend how to do it.

☐ I'm nearly there, but I need a little more time to really get it.

Multiplication mysteries

Something is puzzling the friends of Ladybird Class. Can you help them work out these multiplication mysteries?

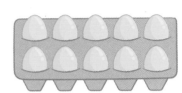
My egg box has 2 rows of 5 eggs. Can you finish my number sentence?

$2 \times 5 = \boxed{}$

My box of eggs has 5 rows of 2 eggs. Can you finish my number sentence?

$5 \times 2 = \boxed{}$

Zara Penguin and Ali Lion both have the same number of eggs, but the number sentences are different. 5×2 makes the same answer as 2×5.

I can see 3 rows of 5 buns. That's 3 lots of 5. Can you fill in my number sentence?

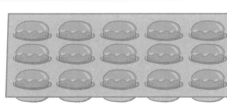

$\boxed{} \times \boxed{} = \boxed{}$

But I can see 5 rows of 3 buns. That's 5 lots of 3. Can you fill in my number sentence?

$\boxed{} \times \boxed{} = \boxed{}$

Tao Meerkat and Noah Panda both have the same number of buns. 3×5 is the same as 5×3.

I can see 2 rows of 10 cabbages. That's 2 lots of 10. Fill in my number sentence.

$$\boxed{} \times \boxed{} = \boxed{}$$

But I can see 10 rows of 2 cabbages. That's 10 lots of 2. Can you fill in my number sentence?

$$\boxed{} \times \boxed{} = \boxed{}$$

Let's draw 10 jumps of 2 on the number line below. That's 10 × 2.

Then use a different colour and draw 2 big jumps of 10. That's 2 × 10.

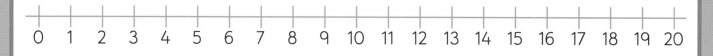

0 1 2 3 4 5 6 7 8 9 10 11 12 13 14 15 16 17 18 19 20

Wow! Both sets of jumps landed on the same number.

So when you multiply two numbers together, they can swap places without changing the answer!

Feeding time

Ladybird Class are feeding the animals. Can you help them share the food fairly?

How many goats do we have to feed? And how many cabbages do we have for them?

Draw a line from one cabbage to a goat. Do the same thing again and again until you have no cabbages left.

There are ⬜ goats. There are ⬜ cabbages.

⬜ cabbages shared between ⬜ goats is ⬜ each.

We need to share these turnips fairly between the sheep, please.

There are ☐ sheep. There are ☐ turnips.

☐ turnips shared between ☐ sheep is ☐ each.

How do we share the biscuits fairly between the dogs?

There are ☐ dogs. There are ☐ biscuits.

☐ biscuits shared between ☐ dogs is ☐ each.

Dividing the picnic

Ladybird Class are having a picnic. Can you help them share the food out fairly between the friends?

We can have one each, and then if there are enough apples, we can have another one each.

Draw lines to share these apples out fairly.

☐ apples shared fairly between ☐ friends is ☐ each.

There is a shorter way of writing "shared fairly between". It is a sign. It looks like this:

$$4 \div 2 = 2$$

This ÷ sign means **shared fairly between** or **divided by**.

26

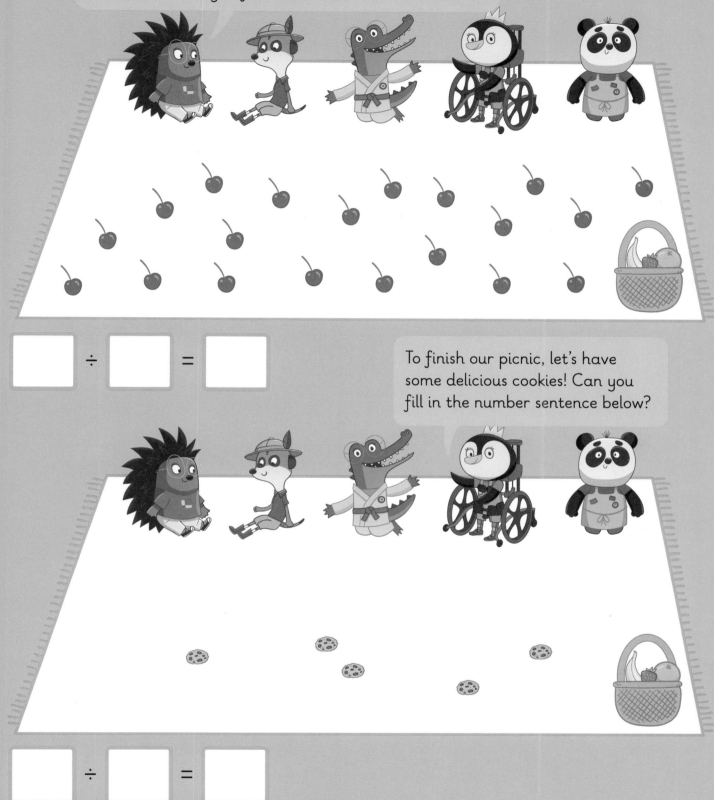

$$\boxed{} \div \boxed{} = \boxed{}$$

$$\boxed{} \div \boxed{} = \boxed{}$$

How are you doing?

How do you feel about dividing numbers fairly?

☐ I'm feeling confident about dividing numbers. It seems fair!

☐ I'm starting to understand how to do it, but I need a bit more help.

Tao Meerkat's magic show

Come and see Tao Meerkat's magic show, as he shuffles numbers to make new number sentences appear!

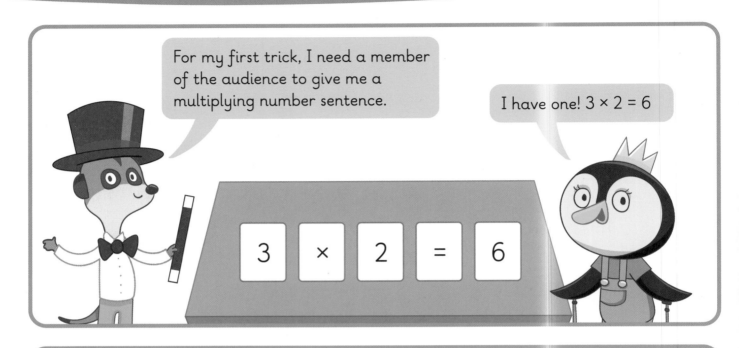

For my first trick, I need a member of the audience to give me a multiplying number sentence.

I have one! 3 × 2 = 6

3 × 2 = 6

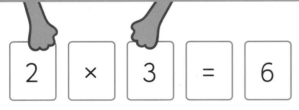

2 × 3 = 6

This is the number sentence that Zara gave me . . . but watch closely. With a magic shuffle, I can make a new number sentence appear!

That's fantastic, Tao! You swapped the 2 and the 3 around and the number sentence still works.

If you swap the two numbers that you are multiplying together, is the answer still the same? Try it to find out.

2 × 5 =   5 × 2 =

10 × 2 =   2 × 10 =

5 × 10 =   10 × 5 =

And now, for my next trick! By using a "division" card, I can make 4 number sentences appear, using only 3 numbers!

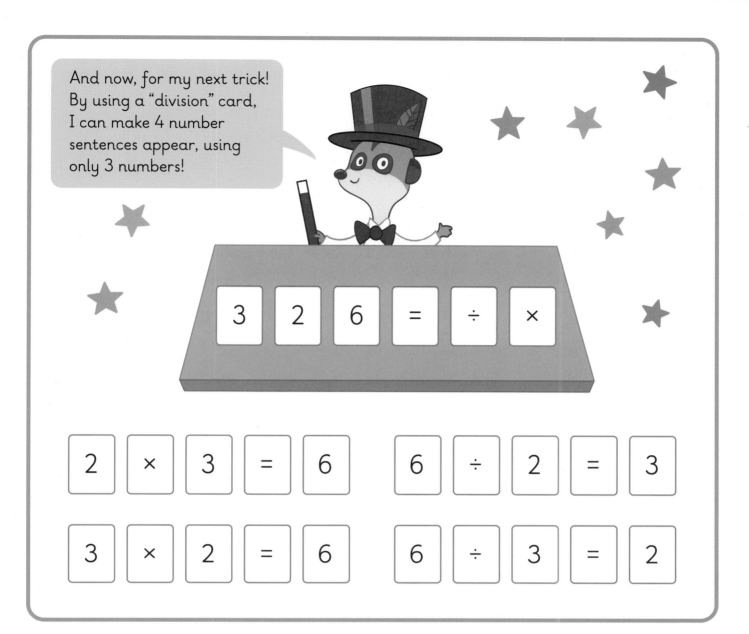

| 3 | 2 | 6 | = | ÷ | × |

| 2 | × | 3 | = | 6 |

| 6 | ÷ | 2 | = | 3 |

| 3 | × | 2 | = | 6 |

| 6 | ÷ | 3 | = | 2 |

Find out which sums you can make using numbers 4, 5 and 20. Fill in these number sentences.

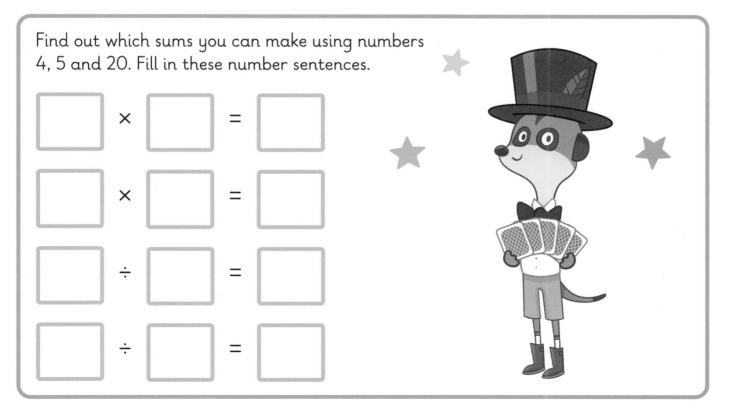

☐ × ☐ = ☐

☐ × ☐ = ☐

☐ ÷ ☐ = ☐

☐ ÷ ☐ = ☐

The Monster Volcano trail

Follow the monster prints on this challenging trail to practise multiplying numbers. The first player to reach Monster Volcano wins!

How to play

1 You need a dice and two counters. Make your own counters with paper or use buttons or little toys. Play with a friend or make the counters play against each other.

2 Place the counters on **Start** and take turns rolling the dice to move forward.

3 If you land on a purple monster print, complete the challenge.

4 The first counter to reach Monster Volcano is the winner!

Number	Challenge	Answer
9	A monster has 2 ears on each of its 2 heads. How many ears does it have altogether?	
16	What is 3 lots of 5?	
25	If a monster has 5 arms, how many arms would 6 monsters have?	
32	Share 8 bones between 2 monsters. How many bones do the monsters have each?	
40	A baby monster has 5 toes on each of its 4 legs. How many toes does it have?	
48	2 monsters have 5 noses each. How many noses do they have altogether?	
55	If a monster has 6 spikes on their back, how many spikes would 2 monsters have?	
62	What is 4×10?	
73	There are 2 baby monsters in each monster nest. How many baby monsters are there in 7 monster nests?	
79	What is 10 divided by 2?	
89	A monster has 12 feet. How many pairs of socks do they need?	
94	What is $100 \div 10$?	

Let's go, Zara! Follow the monster prints with me.

The winner can have these yummy jellies!

Start

Finish!

31

Answers

Pages 4–5
Counting caterpillars
Caterpillar rows
2, 4, 6, 8, 10
Counting in 2s
1, 2, 3, 4, 5, 6, 7, 8, 9, 10, 11,
12, 13, 14, 15, 16, 17, 18, 19, 20

Pages 6–7
More counting in 2s
Boots
2, 4, 6, 8, 10, 12, 14, 16, 18, 20
Gloves
2, 4, 6, 8, 10, 12, 14, 16, 18, 20, 22, 24
Buns
2, 4, 6, 8, 10, 12, 14, 16, 18, 20
Noah Panda will need 10 bags.
Socks
Ali Lion has 12 pairs of socks.

Pages 8–9
How many 2s
Counting legs

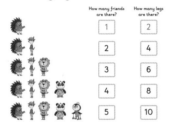

1 friend has 2 legs.
2 friends have 4 legs.
3 friends have 6 legs.
4 friends have 8 legs.
5 friends have 10 legs.
Multiplying by 2

$4 \times 2 = 8$	$9 \times 2 = 18$
$5 \times 2 = 10$	$10 \times 2 = 20$
$6 \times 2 = 12$	$11 \times 2 = 22$
$7 \times 2 = 14$	$12 \times 2 = 24$
$8 \times 2 = 16$	

Pages 10–11
Counting in 5s
Petals
5, 10, 15, 20, 25, 30, 35, 40, 45, 50
Balloons
$5 \times 5 = 25$
Multiplying by 5

$4 \times 5 = 20$	$9 \times 5 = 45$
$5 \times 5 = 25$	$10 \times 5 = 50$
$6 \times 5 = 30$	$11 \times 5 = 55$
$7 \times 5 = 35$	$12 \times 5 = 60$
$8 \times 5 = 40$	

Pages 12–13
The multiplying market
Fruit and vegetables
4 trays of bananas = 20 bananas
6 trays of tomatoes = 30 tomatoes
5 trays of oranges = 10 oranges

3 trays of apples = 15 apples
9 trays of onions = 18 onions
8 trays of carrots = 16 carrots
The ice-cream stall
Zara Penguin: $2 \times 2p = 4p$
Ali Lion: $3 \times 2p = 6p$
Tao Meerkat: $4 \times 5p = 20p$
Nia Hedgehog: $2 \times 5p + 2p = 12p$ altogether
Noah Panda: $2 \times 5p + 5p = 15p$ altogether
Olivia Crocodile: $5 \times 5p = 25p$ altogether
Olivia spent the most money.

Pages 14–15
The daisy-chain game
Count the daisies
100 daisies
The longest daisy chain
Noah Panda's special daisy is number 100.

Pages 18–19
Number-line jumps
2s
1 jump of 2 landed at 2; $1 \times 2 = 2$
2 jumps of 2 landed at 4; $2 \times 2 = 4$
3 jumps of 2 landed at 6; $3 \times 2 = 6$
4 jumps of 2 landed at 8; $4 \times 2 = 8$
5 jumps of 2 landed at 10; $5 \times 2 = 10$
6 jumps of 2 landed at 12; $6 \times 2 = 12$
5s
1 jump of 5 landed at 5; $1 \times 5 = 5$
2 jumps of 5 landed at 10; $2 \times 5 = 10$
3 jumps of 5 landed at 15; $3 \times 5 = 15$
4 jumps of 5 landed at 20; $4 \times 5 = 20$
5 jumps of 5 landed at 25; $5 \times 5 = 25$
6 jumps of 5 landed at 30; $6 \times 5 = 30$
10s
1 jump of 10 landed at 10; $1 \times 10 = 10$
2 jumps of 10 landed at 20; $2 \times 10 = 20$
3 jumps of 10 landed at 30; $3 \times 10 = 30$
4 jumps of 10 landed at 40; $4 \times 10 = 40$
5 jumps of 10 landed at 50; $5 \times 10 = 50$
6 jumps of 10 landed at 60; $6 \times 10 = 60$

Pages 20–21
Number patterns
100-square patterns

1	2	3	4	⑤	6	7	8	9	⑩
11	12	13	14	⑮	16	17	18	19	⑳
21	22	23	24	㉕	26	27	28	29	㉚
31	32	33	34	㉟	36	37	38	39	㊵
41	42	43	44	㊺	46	47	48	49	㊿
51	52	53	54	55	56	57	58	59	60
61	62	63	64	65	66	67	68	69	70
71	72	73	74	75	76	77	78	79	80
81	82	83	84	85	86	87	88	89	90
91	92	93	94	95	96	97	98	99	100

10, 20, 30, 40, 50, 60, 70, 80, 90, 100
Join the dots

Pages 22–23
Multiplication mysteries
Egg boxes
$2 \times 5 = 10$ $5 \times 2 = 10$

The bun tray
$5 \times 3 = 15$ $3 \times 5 = 15$
The cabbage patch
$10 \times 2 = 20$ $2 \times 10 = 20$
Number-line jumps

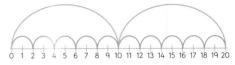

Pages 24–25
Feeding time
Cabbages for the goats
There are 4 goats. There are 8 cabbages.
8 cabbages shared between 4 goats is 2 each.
Turnips for the sheep
There are 5 sheep. There are 10 turnips.
10 turnips shared between 5 sheep is 2 each.
Biscuits for the sheepdogs
There are 2 dogs. There are 12 biscuits.
12 biscuits shared between 2 dogs is 6 each.

Pages 26–27
Dividing the picnic
Apples
10 apples shared between 5 is 2 each.
Cherries
20 cherries shared between 5 is 4 each.
$20 \div 5 = 4$
Cookies
5 cookies shared between 5 is 1 each.
$5 \div 5 = 1$

Pages 28–29
Tao Meerkat's magic show
Shuffle surprise

$2 \times 5 = 10$	$5 \times 2 = 10$
$10 \times 2 = 20$	$2 \times 10 = 20$
$5 \times 10 = 50$	$10 \times 5 = 50$

Division magic

$4 \times 5 = 20$	$20 \div 5 = 4$
$5 \times 4 = 20$	$20 \div 4 = 5$

Pages 30–31
The Monster Volcano trail
Footprint 9: 4
Footprint 16: 15
Footprint 25: 30
Footprint 32: 4
Footprint 40: 20
Footprint 48: 10
Footprint 55: 12
Footprint 62: 40
Footprint 73: 14
Footprint 79: 5
Footprint 89: 6
Footprint 94: 10